Messe Solennelle
(ST. CECILIA)

for

**SOPRANO, TENOR, AND BASS SOLI
AND FULL CHORUS OF MIXED VOICES
WITH PIANO OR ORGAN ACCOMPANIMENT**

by

Charles Gounod

Edited and Piano Accompaniment
Arranged by
JOSEPH BARNBY

Ed. 407

G. SCHIRMER, Inc.

DISTRIBUTED BY

HAL•LEONARD®
CORPORATION
7777 W. BLUEMOUND RD. P.O. BOX 13819 MILWAUKEE, WI 53213

Gounod's "Messe Solennelle."
(St. Cecilia.)
Nº 1. Kyrie.

13

Nº 2. Gloria in excelsis.

De - o, et in ter - ra pax ho - mi - ni - bus, bo - næ, bo - næ, bonæ vo - lun -
High - est, and on earth peace to mankind, peace and good will be to man up -

ta - tis,
on earth,

Glo - ri - a in ex - cel - sis De - o, Glo - ri - a in ex - cel - sis,
Glo - rious is Thy name Je - ho - vah, Glo - rious in the High - est,

Glo - ri - a in ex - cel - sis De - o, Glo - ri - a in ex - cel - sis,
Glo - rious is Thy name Je - ho - vah, Glo - rious in the High - est,

Allegro pomposo.

Tenor Solo.

Pa - - - tris: qui tol - lis, qui tol - lis pec - ca - ta mun - di, mi - se - re - re__ no - bis, mi - se - re - re__ no - - bis.

Fa - - ther Who tak - est up - on thee the sins of the world:___ grant us thy sal - va - tion, grant us thy sal - va - - tion.

qui tol - lis, qui tol - lis pec - ca - ta mun - di: su - sci - pe__ de - pre - ca - ti -
Thou that tak - est up - on thee re - demp - tion of mor - tals, pit - y us,___ vis - it us__ with

su - sci - pe, su - sci - pe de - pre - ca - ti -
Pit - y us, pit - y us, vis - it us__ with

Soprano Solo.

30

№ 3. Credo.

36

*) This Movement should be sung by the Choirs as *piano* as possible.

42

44

46

50

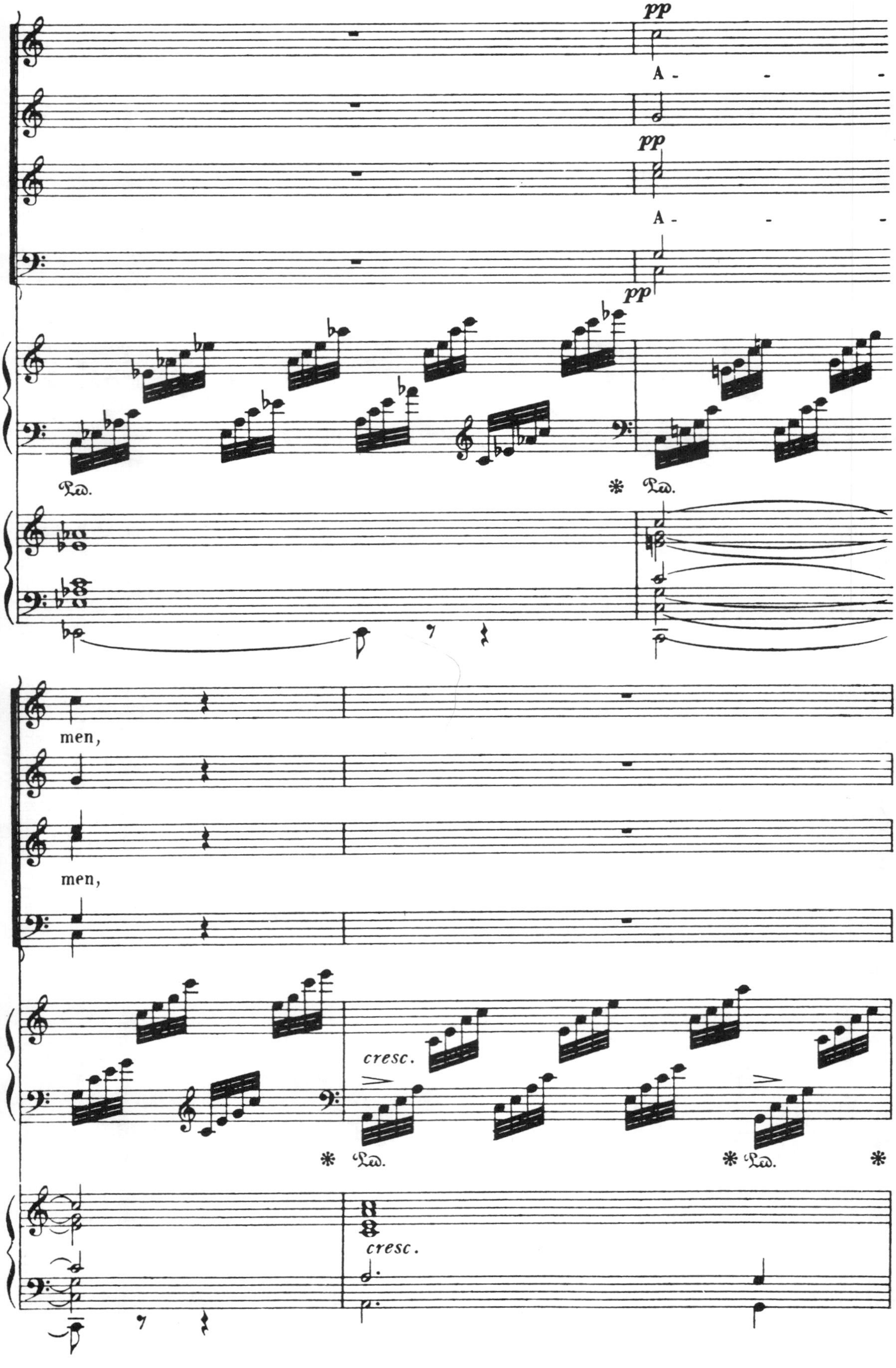
pp
A - - -
pp
A - - -
pp
Ped.
*
Ped.
men,
men,
cresc.
*
Ped.
*
Ped.
*
cresc.

Offertory.

(ORGAN.)

Nº 4. Sanctus.

Tenor Solo.

№ 5. Benedictus.

Nº 6. Agnus Dei.

cem. _____   A - men,   A - men,
tion. _____   A - men,   A - men,

cem. _____   A - men,   A - men,
tion. _____   A - men,   A - men,

A - - - - men. _____
A - - - - men. _____

A - - - - men. _____
A - - - - men. _____